M000015362

I'M ANXIOUS

Philip De Courcy

Consulting Editor: Dr. Paul Tautges

Help! I'm Anxious

© 2018 Philip De Courcy

ISBN
Paper: 978-1-63342-133-2
epub: 978-1-63342-134-9
Kindle: 978-1-63342-136-6

Published by **Shepherd Press**
P.O. Box 24
Wapwallopen, PA 18660

www.shepherdpress.com

Scripture quotes are from the NKJV.

Designed by **documen**

CONTENTS

INTRODUCTION

A woman visited her doctor and told him she was not feeling like herself but was rather run down. After listening to her describe her many symptoms, and then examining her, the doctor replied, "Ma'am, it's my expert opinion that you are not run down, but all wound up." All joking aside, this describes a lot of people—all tied up in the knots of anxiety.

Proverbs 12:25 describes reality:

Anxiety in the heart of man causes depression,
But a good word makes it glad.

Therefore, it should be no surprise that an increasing number of us are worrying ourselves sick. We're worried about an unforgiven past, an untidy present, or an unknown future. We're worried about losing our house to the bank, our job to a multinational corporation overseas, our children to an immoral culture, our sons and daughters to war, our freedoms to activist judges, our spouse to another, our life to cancer, and our faith to unbelief.

Perhaps you know someone like this. Perhaps this describes you.

As a society, we're also consuming an ever-increasing amount of medication alongside more frequent visits to therapists and counselors. Since this is true, it is important to clarify right from the start that the purpose of this mini-book is to bring biblical counsel to your heart. Though sometimes there are medical issues related to anxiety, I'm addressing anxiety from a biblical perspective only, not a medical one. If you are having severe anxiety attacks, you should see your family physician for a medical checkup. My role is to be a physician of the soul only, to help apply the comforting and challenging truths of God's Word to your mind and heart so that you may experience spiritual peace.

To one degree or another, we all worry; we all wrestle with anxiety. And Jesus knew it would be this way. That's why he devoted a large amount of the most famous sermon in history to the subject. One in seven words in the Sermon on the Mount (Matthew 5–7) addresses how you and I can have victory over worry. For Jesus, this was an immediate and important matter. He did not want his disciples held captive by the regret of yesterday, the pressures of today, and the fears of tomorrow. Jesus wants his people to be as free as the proverbial birds of the air, and to entrust themselves fully into the caring hands of their heavenly Father. Therefore, Jesus speaks counsel to our hearts.

In this mini-book, we will look at the Master's teaching on anxiety from the Sermon on the Mount. I encourage you to open your ears and heart to listen to Jesus. Press the Pause button. Take a moment to ask God to speak words of peace and comfort to your anxious heart.

at's Wrong with Anxiety?

In 1994, my wife and I moved our family from our native Northern Ireland to the United States of America. As we anticipated our move across the Atlantic Ocean, we happened to be reading *The Message* by Eugene Peterson. When we got to the sixth chapter of the Gospel of Matthew, one key verse with the words of Jesus spoke to our hearts:

> Look at the birds, free and unfettered, not tied down to a job description, careless in the care of God.
>
> *(Matthew 6:26)*

Immediately we latched onto the phrase "careless in the care of God," and the Holy Spirit used it to calm our nerves concerning the magnitude of this move across the pond. Having sensed the Lord's call to further theological training at The Master's Seminary, we gathered our belongings and three young daughters and boarded a plane to leave behind everything familiar. We left behind all that brought a sense of security to our lives. But, by faith, we could now move forward carefree (uncontrolled by worry) because our hearts were fixed on being "careless in the care of God."

To be sure, "careless in the care of God" does not equal reckless abandonment. When Jesus tells us not to worry, he isn't encouraging us to be careless in the sense that we do not plan, work, or think about our everyday concerns. In this respect the King James Version's translation of this passage is sometimes misunderstood, since it reads "Take . . . no thought for the morrow" (Matthew 6:34). But thinking about tomorrow, and planning for it, isn't condemned by Jesus. So what does Jesus mean? Essentially, Jesus says the same thing as his half-brother James said later. Instead of arrogantly boasting about what we plan to do tomorrow, we

> ought to say, "If the Lord wills, we shall live and do this or that."
>
> (James 4:15)

In other words, faith involves humbly submitting *tomorrow* to God's good and sovereign will, while we live out *today* in obedience.

As the old hymn says, this is our Father's world; therefore he pays special attention to his children and their needs. So let's begin by listening to Jesus describe our heavenly Father's care in the key passage of Scripture we will work through together.

> ²⁴No one can serve two masters; for either
> he will hate the one and love the other,
> or else he will be loyal to the one and
> despise the other. You cannot serve God
> and mammon.
> ²⁵Therefore I say to you, do not worry about
> your life, what you will eat or what you
> will drink; nor about your body, what you
> will put on. Is not life more than food and
> the body more than clothing? ²⁶Look at
> the birds of the air, for they neither sow
> nor reap nor gather into barns; yet your
> heavenly Father feeds them. Are you not of
> more value than they? ²⁷Which of you by
> worrying can add one cubit to his stature?
> ²⁸So why do you worry about clothing?
> Consider the lilies of the field, how they
> grow: they neither toil nor spin; ²⁹and yet
> I say to you that even Solomon in all his
> glory was not arrayed like one of these.
> ³⁰Now if God so clothes the grass of the
> field, which today is, and tomorrow is
> thrown into the oven, will He not much

more clothe you, *O you of little faith?*
³¹*Therefore do not worry, saying, "What*
shall we eat?" or "What shall we drink?"
or "What shall we wear?" ³²*For after all*
these things the Gentiles seek. For your
heavenly Father knows that you need all
these things. ³³*But seek first the kingdom*
of God and His righteousness, and all
these things shall be added to you.
³⁴*Therefore do not worry about tomorrow, for*
tomorrow will worry about its own things.
Sufficient for the day is its own trouble.
(Matthew 6:24–34)

Notice how Jesus introduces the issue of anxiety by confronting the subtle ways we shift our heart's allegiance from trusting God to trusting in earthly securities such as material provision.

Who Is Your Master?

You may have noticed verse 25 begins with the word "therefore," which means "for this reason." This links what Jesus is about to say with what he just said about laying up treasure for ourselves on earth instead of in heaven and therefore challenges his audience to choose whom they will serve: God or money. The point here is that if we follow God as our Master, treasure the gospel, and invest in heaven, we may be tempted to ask, "Who will take care of my needs here and now, on this earth?" Jesus anticipates this question and therefore goes on to say, in effect, "Treasure the Lord. Rest in him as your security. Seek him first. Value his kingdom above all. Let thoughts of heaven govern your mind. When you do so, God will take care of your material needs."

In contrast, when we make money our master, anxiety cracks the whip in order to keep us hoarding for the future. If money is our god, we will always worry about whether we have enough for tomorrow, and we will endeavor to keep what we gain today. That's why people who have more money tend to have more worries about money. Leon Morris is onto something when he writes in his commentary on Matthew,

> *The new thought here is that we can be unfaithful to God and unfruitful in life through care as much as covetousness.*[1]

In other words, the ongoing presence of anxiety may indicate that our trust is in stockpiling possessions, rather than in worshipping God.

Recognizing Worry

Worry is the key word in these verses. Six times Jesus uses it to identify the problem as real—one we wrestle with daily. We struggle with insecurity regarding tomorrow and insufficiency regarding today. This tendency to be anxious, alongside the temptation to trust money rather than God, was also a real struggle for those who first heard Jesus preach.

The average Jew of that day lived in subjection to the Romans. He may have had to pay as much as 40 percent of his income in taxes. On top of that, he was hired and compensated on a daily basis. Consequently, if he didn't get paid at the end of each day, his family would immediately feel the effect. There would be no bread on the table or milk in the jug. In addition, since they lived in a region which was plagued by drought and famine, their mere existence was in constant jeopardy! So the question anticipated by Jesus was real: "Where will I get what I need to eat, drink, and wear?"

As the Son of Man, Jesus understood their struggle. He was from a working-class family in a blue-collar town. He knew all about the daily stress of ordinary folks who struggled to make ends meet. We see this in the Gospels. Jesus talks about clothes needing to be patched (Mark 2:21), a woman sweeping her house to find a lost coin (Luke 15:8), and bargains that could be found at the market—"two sparrows sold for a copper coin" (Matthew 10:29). Jesus spoke to people who had good reason to worry, yet he didn't give them a pass just because of their socioeconomic disadvantage. Instead Jesus said, "I say to you, do not worry." That's a command. The fact that the Lord Jesus knew about everyday stress makes his prohibition of worry even more striking and convicting for you and me.

Worry Is Distraction

In our day in the Western world, however, we're a step or two removed from this state. As tough as times may get, I doubt that few if any of us wake up on a given day and wonder what we're going to put on our bodies or in our stomachs. So what exactly is worry? If anxiety is the problem Jesus attacks, we need to understand what it is. The word translated "worry" means "to be divided in your mind." Jesus is saying, "Don't be distracted and torn up inside about what you're going to eat, drink, and wear." Essentially, to be anxious is to be distracted, torn in different directions.

The same word is used to describe Martha when she got all wound up about her sister not helping to prepare dinner for Jesus. When Jesus spoke to her, he had to say her name twice because she was so anxious:

> Martha, Martha, you are worried and
> troubled about many things.
>
> *(Luke 10:41)*

"You're troubled" is from the same word for "worry." Martha was worried about many things, but Jesus told her that "only one thing" was really needed: that which Mary had chosen—to sit at his feet and learn from him (Luke 10:42). Martha had lost her focus and, as a result, became overwhelmed by the situation she found herself in. Her divided mind and heart led to her desperate state. That's how anxiety works.

Anxiety takes our energy and divides it between today's pressures and priorities and tomorrow's problems and possibilities. This leads to one part of our mind being preoccupied with the here-and-now, and the other part by the there-and-not-yet. It means we're double-minded, which can result in our being halfhearted about what is most important. When we are overcome with anxiety, we cannot give our whole self to the moment because part of us is "somewhere else." Maybe it's a health report, a job opportunity, or a business deal that's hanging in the balance. Whatever *it* is, it divides our mind, diffuses our energies, and distracts us from giving ourselves to what needs our attention the most.

Good Worry, Bad Worry

There is, however, an important distinction we need to make. As stated above, living without worry does not mean being reckless. There *are* matters that *ought* to concern us, things that deserve our immediate attention and action. Being carefree is not the same as being careless.

The Greek word for "worry" in Matthew 6 is sometimes used elsewhere to convey legitimate concern for something or someone. In fact, this word is used by the apostle Paul to describe the mental and pastoral weight he carried daily, his "deep concern for all the churches" (2 Corinthians 11:28). He also used the word to describe Timothy's sincere "care" for the spiritual growth of believers in the city of Philippi (Philippians 2:20). We should, therefore, sometimes express intense care and concern for the advancement of the Lord's work and the welfare of his people. There is such a thing as good worry and appropriate anxiety. We *should* be concerned about the welfare of our nation, the state of our own souls, the health of the church, the peril of the lost, the future of our children, and the care of our aged parents. The Christian is not a happy-go-lucky kind of character who breezes through life with a thoughtless attitude and naïve approach to living for God. So what does Jesus prohibit?

Practical Atheism

Jesus gives the command abruptly to his followers: "Therefore I say to you, do not worry." There are no "ifs" or "buts": this is a command to immediately refrain from worrying. The construction of the Greek here carries the idea that those listening to the sermon had already given themselves over to worry and that Jesus is therefore telling them to immediately stop being anxious. This is a blanket ban on "bad worry." Bad worry is inappropriate in light of God's promises, providence, and power.

The apostle Paul repeats this imperative in Philippians 4:6:

Be anxious for nothing, but in everything

> by prayer and supplication, with thanks-
> giving, let your requests be made known
> to God.

Anxious care, or illegitimate concern, is out of place in the company of Christians and certainly in the presence of God. Anxiety is not a personality trait or culturally accepted norm, but a violation of God's will for which we need forgiveness. However, too often we treat worry as a "respectable sin."[2] When you and I worry, we are being disobedient. We are sinning. I believe it was John Wesley who said, "I can no more worry than I can curse or swear."

Anxiety takes God out of the picture, causing us to respond to a situation as if he were not present. That's what I mean by *practical atheism*: we are thinking and living as if God has vacated the throne of heaven. Clearly, then, anxiety is no small sin. But not only that, it is not a solitary sin; it spawns others. Worry is a sin that gives birth to ugly offspring.

Let me give one example. Let's say you worry about your financial security. If you're not careful, worrying about your finances will trigger other sins, such as covetousness of others and discontentment regarding God's providence in your life. But Jesus wants us to be worry-free.

He tells us to stop worrying about whatever is worrying us.

Remember, with Jesus' commands comes his enablement to grow in grace. He doesn't command us to do something that he is not willing to strengthen us to do. You see that principle at work in the story of the man with the withered hand being asked by Jesus to stretch it forth (Mark 3:1–6). Humanly speaking, that would have been impossible, but with any divine commandment comes divine enablement. Therefore, don't say, "I *can't* stop worrying." You can, and you must. And by God's grace, you will.

2

Reasons Not to Be Anxious

One Sunday morning, as he was leaving the worship service, a man said, "Pastor, don't tell me that worry doesn't work. I've worried about lots of things and they've never happened." I think the man was missing the point! Worry doesn't change a thing, but it does change us—and for the worse, not the better. Worry is a fruitless and frustrating exercise. As we continue to listen to Jesus preach against anxiety we hear him give three reasons not to allow worry to control us.

Anxiety Is Senseless

According to Jesus, anxiety is useless, pointless, and senseless. Here's what he says to us when we are worried:

> Look at the birds of the air, for they neither sow nor reap nor gather into barns; yet your heavenly Father feeds them. Are you not of more value than they? Which of you by

worrying can add one cubit to his stature?

(Matthew 6:26–27)

Some Bible scholars argue that "stature" is better translated "life span." I agree. Worry is a lot of work for nothing. When we worry, we expend physical, mental, and emotional energy while receiving no benefits. In fact, anxiety typically does the opposite. Rather than lengthen our lives to any degree, anxiety shortens them. Though we may worry with our minds, our bodies often suffer. It also weakens our ability to deal properly with the very thing we're concerned about. Worry divides and drains us, thereby immobilizing us. Jesus points out that stressing over things outside our control is senseless. Instead, we can and must trust God to provide.

James 1:17 assures us,

Every good gift and every perfect gift is from above, and comes down from the Father of lights, with whom there is no variation or shadow of turning.

My unmarried daughters know that, as much as I am able, I will do all I can to meet their needs with the resources I have. But they also know that their earthly father's resources are limited. Our heavenly Father is different, though. He is the giver of every good and perfect gift, and he never changes. He never fails. Are you anxious about your needs? God is working to meet them. And remember, his resources are infinite. Omnipotence is working for you!

Anxiety Is Sinful

Anxiety is not only senseless, it's sinful, because Jesus directly prohibits it. Here's another angle of approach:

> Now if God so clothes the grass of the field,
> which today is, and tomorrow is thrown
> into the oven, will He not much more
> clothe you, O you of little faith?
>
> *(Matthew 6:30)*

According to Jesus, worry is a fruit of unbelief. The disciples were clearly deficient in their trust of God: "O you of little faith." Jesus expected more from them. They were not resting in God's provision. They were not alive to the providence of God being worked out before their very eyes, day by day, in creation. The birds of the air could have told them not to worry. The flowers of the field would have loved to speak words of assurance to them. But the followers of Jesus lacked faith in the faithfulness of God.

The apostle Paul also gently confronts the subtlety of our unbelief when he writes,

> For whatever is not from faith is sin.
> *(Romans 14:23)*

The author of Hebrews writes similarly:

> But without faith it is impossible to please Him.
> *(Hebrews 11:6)*

Worry is a lack of faith; it dishonors and displeases God. Therefore, it is sin.

Worry has no redeeming quality because the root of anxiety is a failure of faith. It envisions circumstances which may never occur, and forgets truths about God's person and works which have never changed. That's why George Müller, who trusted God to provide for orphanages all across England, said,

> *The beginning of anxiety is the end of faith, and the beginning of true faith is the end of anxiety.*[3]

But we have a great God with enormous resources:

The earth is the LORD's, and all its fullness.

(Psalm 24:1)

God's provisions are powerful and plentiful. He deserves more than little faith, doesn't he?

Vance Havner, a well-loved Bible teacher from the last century, liked to tell the following story. There was a lady who went to the doctor when things were a little too late, medically speaking. After examining her, the doctor said, "Madam, it seems to me you are just going to have to trust the Lord on this." The lady replied in a tone of desperation, "Doctor, has it really come to that?" Havner loved to finish the story with the words, "It always comes to that, and since it does, we might as well start with that! God is not a last resort."[4] If we entrust our souls to God's eternal keeping, can we not entrust our days and difficulties to him also?

Anxiety Is Slanderous

Worry is also a poor witness to a watching world, since it makes us look like unbelievers rather than believers in the Lord. To slander someone means to speak down about that person, to lower others' opinion of him or her. In a similar manner, when we are controlled by worry, we lower others' opinion of God. Jesus says it this way:

> Therefore do not worry, saying, "What shall we eat?" or "What shall we drink?" or "What shall we wear?" For after all these things the Gentiles seek. For your heavenly Father knows that you need all these things.
> (Matthew 6:31–32)

According to Jesus, it's expected that unbelievers will fret and fuss over life's necessities. They run after things. That's what the word "seek" means. Since non-Christians have "their understanding darkened, being alienated from the life of God, because of the ignorance that is in them, because of the blindness of their heart" (Ephesians 4:18), they naturally rely upon themselves. Therefore, among unbelievers there tends to be a fever pitch of activity directed toward securing enough possessions to gain security. Jesus, therefore, is not surprised that they worry; he's just shocked that his disciples worry, acting like orphans in their Father's world. The world may be excused, but not the Christian. The Father knows what the Christian needs, and that should make a difference with regard to the level of anxiety in a Christian.

If we are Christians we should think and act differently because we know that God cares about us and acts on our behalf. First Peter 5:7 exhorts and assures us in the very same sentence:

> . . . casting all your care upon Him, for He cares for you.

The first use of "care" here means "worry." It's the same word Jesus used. Cast your worry, your anxiety, upon God, because he cares for you. The second "care" is a different word. It means that God thinks about you, he cares for you. So cast all your anxieties upon God because he thinks about you. You're his precious child, and he will take care of your needs as you take care of his kingdom. So don't worry.

A Peaceful Heart Is a Powerful Testimony

In contrast to the harmful testimony of an anxious heart, the Christian ought to model the powerful testimony of a peaceful heart. This is seen in the story of John Wesley's conversion to Christ. John Wesley is best known as an Oxford teacher, evangelist, open-air preacher, and one of the fathers of Methodism. But John was a missionary before he became a true Christian. Amazingly, he embarked upon ministry overseas without actually knowing the Lord.

On Sunday, January 25, 1736, Wesley boarded a ship in his native England and set sail for America. While at sea, the sailors encountered a life-threatening storm. Among them were some Moravian Christians from Bohemia (now part of the Czech Republic). In the midst of the storm, these believers were not overcome by fear, but gathered on deck to pray and sing praises to God. While the storm raged and the ship lurched, the hearts of the Moravians remained calm. Struck by this, Wesley recognized that these followers of Christ had something he did not. They had inner peace *with* God. They also experienced the peace *of* God. But he had neither.

Several years later, after an unsuccessful ministry among the Indians in Savannah, Georgia, John returned to England. His spirit was bruised and his heart broken. "I went out to convert the heathen, but who will convert me?" he cried. And the Lord answered.

In his biography, *Wesley and Men Who Followed*, Iain Murray describes John's conversion:

In February 1738 Wesley was back in England,

and a few months later came the great crisis. On 24 May 1738, the best-known incident of his life, he became, as he believed, a real Christian. It happened in a small gathering in Aldersgate Street, London, when someone was reading Luther's Preface to the Epistle to the Romans:

"About a quarter before nine, while he was describing the change which God works in the heart through faith in Christ, I felt my heart strangely warmed. I felt I did trust in Christ, Christ alone for salvation; and an assurance was given me, that He had taken away my sins, even mine, and saved me from the law of sin and death."

From this point Wesley was a changed man. . . . It was what happened to him in the year of his thirty-fifth birthday that made the difference and the effects of the change in him were immediate.

The next month, he preached on Ephesians 2:8, "For by grace you have been saved through faith, and that not of yourselves; it is the gift of God." To his listeners, he explained true salvation as

a deliverance from guilt and punishment, by

the atonement of Christ actually applied to the soul of the sinner now believing on Him, and a deliverance from the power of sin, through Christ formed in his heart. So that he who is thus justified, or saved by faith, is indeed born again. He is born again of the Spirit unto a new life.[5]

What did Wesley come to realize? What had the Holy Spirit opened the eyes of his heart to see? That he was religious but did not have a relationship with the living God; that he was serving God without even knowing God; and that he was trying to live for God, but was spiritually dead and, therefore, needed to be born again by the Holy Spirit through the gospel. Such is the need of each one of us.

What about you? Let me ask you a few important questions:

» How would you describe your relationship with God?

» Do you have religion without relationship?

» Are you trying to live for God without having the life of God resident in your soul?

» Have you been born again?

» Perhaps you know in your head that Jesus Christ is the Savior of the world, but do you believe in your heart that he is *your* Savior?

» Are you trusting in his sin-atoning work on the cross, or in your own attempts to become righteous? Do you know him as *your* living Lord?

There was a time when I did not know Jesus Christ. But when I was sixteen years old, the Lord graciously showed me *my* sinfulness and led *me* to repentance and faith in Jesus as *my* Savior and Lord. And it is my heart's greatest desire that you, too, have assurance of salvation in Jesus Christ. The good news of the gospel to every sinner is simple:

> . . . *if you confess with your mouth the Lord Jesus and believe in your heart that God has raised Him from the dead, you will be saved. For with the heart one believes unto righteousness, and with the mouth confession is made unto salvation. For the Scripture says, "Whoever believes on Him will not be put to shame."*
>
> (Romans 10:9–11)

"What does all of this have to do with anxiety?"

you may be asking. John Wesley's conversion to Christ was triggered by witnessing a group of Christians who displayed peace. They didn't give in to anxiety and slander the character of God before others. Instead, they trusted God with childlike faith. They knew in their hearts that the Creator of that particular storm, on that particular day, was also their heavenly Father. Instead of their minds being controlled by events outside their control, they chose to rest in the faithful character of the One who has all things under control. Instead of their minds being divided, they hurled their cares upon the God who also assures us that, if we are in Christ, we don't need to worry or fear, because he cares for us.

3

Moving Toward a Settled Mind

One of my favorite comic strips is *Peanuts* by Charles Schulz. One day, Linus and Lucy are sitting by the windowsill while it's raining heavily outside. Lucy says to Linus, "You know, if this keeps up we're going to get flooded and swept away." Linus replies, "Lucy, don't be silly. Genesis 9 in the Bible says that God promised that there would be no more floods and that the rainbow in the sky is a reminder that He will keep that promise." Lucy says, "You know what, Linus? You're right, and you know what? I feel a lot better now that you've said that." Linus replies, "Sound doctrine has a way of doing that."[6]

Linus was wiser than many of us realize. Meditating on biblical truth calms our hearts and steadies our minds. On the flipside, worry spreads easily when our minds are not safeguarded by right thinking. You and I sleep more soundly, and live more securely, when we set our minds on the truths of our faithful God who has promised to look after those who are in Christ.

Renewing Our Minds

As we continue to listen to Jesus' sermon, we hear him prescribe the remedy for anxiety. Having diagnosed the underlying problem of unbelief, Jesus proceeds to write a prescription for the worried mind. He fundamentally seeks to renew the disciples' minds by grounding them in the truth about God and his relationship to them. We find this theme throughout the Word of God.

For example, the prophet Isaiah says,

> You will keep him in perfect peace,
> Whose mind is stayed on You,
> Because he trusts in You.
>
> *(Isaiah 26:3)*

The apostle Paul also assures us that peace comes to those who submit their minds to God:

> Be anxious for nothing, but in everything
> by prayer and supplication, with
> thanksgiving, let your requests be made
> known to God; and the peace of God,

which surpasses all understanding, will
guard [and garrison] your hearts and
minds through Christ Jesus.

(Philippians 4:6–7)

Notice, though, that the apostle immediately reveals that this peace does not come to the passive mind, but to the mind that is actively being renewed by truth:

Finally, brethren, whatever things are true,
whatever things are noble, whatever things
are just, whatever things are pure, whatever
things are lovely, whatever things are of
good report, if there is any virtue and if
there is anything praiseworthy—meditate
on these things.

(4:8)

In other words, when we intentionally think about these qualities (v. 8), the peace of God becomes our security guard (v. 7). A stable mind thinks biblically; it rests upon the sure foundation of God's Word. In contrast, to a large measure, we become anxious Christians when we are not thinking straight, when our thinking is not aligned with sound theology. Sinclair Ferguson writes,

Jesus' teaching then is not a form of the
power of positive thinking. The problem
with anxious people is not merely that they
think negatively about life. The problem
is much more radical than that. Anxious
people do not think theologically about
life. Their problem is not that they have
low self-images. The problem is that in all
their thoughts there is no room for God
(Psalm 10:4). It is only when their focus
upon God is restored that they can finally
experience the conquest of anxiety.[7]

Put another way, we get anxious when we allow
our minds to dwell on things that are not God-
centered or Christ-exalting. We worry when our
minds are divided between faith and unbelief,
between today and tomorrow.

Moving toward a mind settled upon truth
requires two steps.

Step 1: Reassess Your Value System

First, Jesus prescribes a reassessment. He asks, "Is
not life more than food and the body more than
clothing?" (Matthew 6:25). And then he directs
them to "Look at the birds of the air." Why? He
explains, "Your heavenly Father feeds them. Are

you not of more value than they?" (v. 26). Then he adds,

> *Consider the lilies of the field, how they grow . . . and yet I say to you that even Solomon in all his glory was not arrayed like one of these. Now if God so clothes the grass of the field, which today is, and tomorrow is thrown into the oven, will He not much more clothe you, O you of little faith?*
>
> *(vv. 28–30)*

His argument is simple: worry arises when we put high price tags on the wrong things. In essence, Jesus corrects his listeners for overvaluing the temporal and undervaluing the eternal. They were worried about food and clothing instead of about their life and walk with God. So they needed to reassess their values. They needed a fresh understanding of what God treasures, and they needed to be convinced of their own value to God. If they really grasped these, they would cease their fussing and fretting. To this end, Jesus applied logic.

From the Greater to the Lesser

In the tradition of a Jewish rabbi, Jesus employs the standard "how much more" argument. He argues from the greater to the lesser in regard to life and food, then he turns that argument on its head and argues from the lesser to the greater in relationship to man and the surrounding creation. He wants his listeners to see that some things are more important than others and to believe that they themselves are most important to God. Why should they worry when they are valuable to God, when their heavenly Father has promised to take care of his children?

If God gave us life, will he not give us the things necessary for life (v. 25)? Why would he give us life, but not give us food to sustain it? Why would he give us a body, but not provide clothes? If he does the greater thing, will he not do the lesser thing? Of course he will!

This principle became clear to me many years ago in a jewelry store in Belfast, when I purchased my wife's engagement ring. After I shelled out the money, I asked the lady behind the counter, "Do I get a box with it?" After first looking at me as if I was the village idiot, she then smiled and said, "Yes, sir. Of course! You're buying a ring. We'll give you a box." It was as if she was saying, "Since you're spending this amount of money, we'll pay the five bucks for the pretty little box to put it in, for you to give to your sweetheart." The one included the other. What jeweler wouldn't give you a cheap box if you bought an expensive ring? It's the same argument that Jesus makes here. If God gives us life, will he not also give us what is necessary to live that life for his glory?

From the Lesser to the Greater

Then Jesus reverses the argument, moving from the lesser to the greater. He draws from the surrounding creation and says, in effect, "Hold on a minute, guys. Here you are worrying about what you're going to eat, but look at the birds of the air. They're not worried about what they're going to eat; your heavenly Father feeds them. And you guys are worried about what you're going to wear? If you'd just look at the meadows and consider the beauty of the lilies, you'd recognize how God has graced his creation with a splash of color. The beauty and the appeal of these far outweigh Solomon and all his splendor! The flowers don't worry, yet God clothes the field. Even to the grass he gives color—grass which is going to be cut down tomorrow and used to fire up the ovens so the women can cook. So tell me this: What is more important? The birds or you? The lilies of the field or you? Look at the created order and stop worrying!"

If God takes care of the lesser creatures, will he not take care of the greater? Man is the crown of God's creation (Psalm 8). At the end of the sixth day, God made man in his own image to have fellowship with him and to reflect God's glory:

Then God saw everything that He had made, and indeed it was very good.

(Genesis 1:31)

And even though mankind rebelled against God's rule, thus turning the good into bad, God did not abandon them. Even at the point of departure God made the promise of redemption (Genesis 3:15). Even now, God is redeeming sinners through the blood of his Son, Jesus Christ, and sealing believers with the Spirit until the day of redemption (Ephesians 4:30). The redeemed community of believers are the apple of his eye, his treasure, his particular people. He says, "Don't you get it, guys? The God who takes care of the birds of the air and clothes the lilies of the field: are you not worth much more to him than they are? Are you not much more valuable than one of them? Yes, you are! You need to reassess your value system."

Step 2: Remember Your Heavenly Father

Already we've seen that God loves his children more than his pets and garden—that is, nature. If God takes care of the lower creation (nature), will he not take care of the higher creation (human beings)? Jesus' point is this: among those whom God has created are those whom he knows in relationship, as their heavenly Father. Believers are those who should remember his lovingkindness and faithfulness. Therefore, we have no need to be anxious. Our heavenly Father knows what we need.

Worry should not characterize God's children because our heavenly Father will be no less for us than a good earthly father would be for his children. Here Jesus introduces the motif for fatherhood, which is rather striking because God is referred to as Father only fourteen times in the whole of the Old Testament, and not one of those mentions is personal. They're all in reference to God's love for the corporate nation of Israel, which is called God's son.

Nonetheless, by the time we get to the New Testament, the Jews had begun to speak of God as their Father, but they were still hesitant in doing so. Jesus was the first to ever make the Fatherhood of God essential to prayer and life. In fact, you find that truth sixty times in the Gospels. The point is this: we have a Father who knows the things we need, and like any good earthly father, he'll see to those needs. Psalm 103:13 reminds us,

> As a father pities his children,
> So the LORD pities those who fear Him.

Jesus makes the same comparison in the Gospel of Luke:

> If a son asks for bread from any father
> among you, will he give him a stone? Or if
> he asks for a fish, will he give him a serpent
> instead of a fish? Or if he asks for an egg,
> will he offer him a scorpion? If you then,
> being evil, know how to give good gifts to
> your children, how much more will your
> heavenly Father give the Holy Spirit to
> those who ask Him!
>
> *(Luke 11:11–13)*

Will a good father give his son a serpent if he asks for a fish? No! We've got a heavenly Father who is like a good earthly father multiplied by a million and more. Just as good earthly fathers protect, clothe, forgive, discipline, and lead their families, so God will care for his family.

In fact, we don't even need to inform him about our circumstances. We don't need to rouse him to come to our aid; he is already predisposed to that. He knows our needs before we even tell him, and he can be counted on to faithfully supply our needs in his perfect time.

The story is told of a slave who was brought to America (an ugly scourge in the history of our nation). One particular day, at the harbor in Charleston, SC, this slave stood on the block to be sold. He stood tall, upright, and with such unusual dignity that one of the buyers said to the seller, "He is different. Why?" The seller replied, "Back in Africa, he was the son of a king, and he hasn't forgotten it yet."

If you have turned from your sin to Jesus Christ in faith, you are an adopted son of God, or daughter of the King of kings. Do you believe this? Does it show up in your demeanor? Does it impact your response to the difficulties of life? Your Father is the best father ever. He knows what you need before you even tell him, and he can meet your needs according to his riches in Christ Jesus (Philippians 4:19). Let this comforting truth settle into your mind so that the stability of God's peace will reign in your heart.

4
Seek God's Kingdom First

Baron Fitzgerald had only one son. This son was the sole heir to his father's wealthy estate. Shortly after leaving home, the son tragically and prematurely died. Crushed, the father himself died some years later, leaving behind a treasure trove of art and paintings to be sold at auction. On the appointed day, a large crowd of art collectors assembled, knowing that the auction included some highly prized paintings. When the auctioneer opened the bidding, the first item to be sold was a painting entitled "My Beloved Son." It was a portrait of the baron's only son. However, since it wasn't a masterpiece, it generated little interest on the part of the art collectors present. Sitting among the crowd, however, was the baron's elderly chauffer who had a deep appreciation for the portrait. Moved by his love for both the father and the son, he placed the winning bid for the painting.

As soon as this first sale was complete, the eyes of everyone turned again to the front of the room for the remainder of the collection.

Collectors were now ready to start bidding on "the good stuff." But the attorney lifted the gavel and dropped it. As the gavel hit the table, he said, "The will reads: 'Whoever buys my son's portrait gets it all.' The auction is over." Shock and dismay filled the room. There was only one satisfied customer—the chauffer, who was rewarded for seeking the father's most valuable treasure first.[8] And so it is for believers in Jesus Christ. When we seek first the Son of God and his kingdom, God gives us everything else. That's the way God works. It follows the pattern of his giving heart:

*He who did not spare His own Son, but
delivered Him up for us all, how shall He
not with Him also freely give us all things?*
(Romans 8:32)

When Jesus Christ occupies his rightful place in our lives, and God's glory becomes the chief goal of all we do, we need not worry. If we have the Son, we have it all. When we seek God first, we can rest in his promise to take care of all our needs.

As Jesus wraps up his teaching on anxiety, that is his closing argument. Don't worry. Seek God first. He will take care of you.

For after all these things the Gentiles seek.
For your heavenly Father knows that you
need all these things. But seek first the
kingdom of God and His righteousness,
and all these things shall be added to you.
Therefore, do not worry about tomorrow, for
tomorrow will worry about its own things.
Sufficient for the day is its own trouble.

(Matthew 6:32–34)

It's Time to Refocus

Anxiety distracts us from serving the Lord, so we need to refocus. When God's concerns become our chief concern, our concerns become his concern. Jesus wants us working, not worrying. If we give ourselves in service to his kingdom, we need not worry about today or tomorrow. God underwrites the lives of those who seek his kingdom.

Experiencing victory over worry requires that we learn to replace our little concerns with life's greatest concern—the kingdom of God. The reason why some of us worry so much is because we think too little of God's kingdom. It's not that our concerns are little in the sense that they are petty or unimportant. It's just that, when compared to God's kingdom, they are small. It's like switching to portrait mode on your phone camera. When God's agenda is in the foreground—in primary focus—our personal concerns move to the background, where they become slightly blurred in comparison.

When anxiety overtakes us, we become bound up in the small stuff of life, the passing, transitory things, when we should be focused on the eternal. Jesus is saying, "Look, God has taken care of the birds and the lilies. He has taken care of the tiny transitory parts of creation. But you're much more valuable. You take care of his business, and don't worry about your own." As mentioned previously, I don't mean that in some reckless way. It doesn't mean that you shouldn't do what you need to do to take care of your family, or that you don't need to pray, plan, or work. It just means we need to keep our priorities straight.

We Need Higher Priorities

It's as if Jesus is saying, "Hold on a minute, guys. You've got mixed-up priorities. You're worried about what you're going to eat, drink, and wear? Look, just keep following me. Let's spread the gospel. Let's be concerned about lost souls. Let's expand the borders of the kingdom." Of course there'll be a future, earthly kingdom when Jesus returns, but in the present, he rules a spiritual kingdom in the hearts that are being changed by the gospel of God's grace. If you give yourself to God's business, he will meet your every need along the way. The other things "shall be added to you." But if the lesser things become little gods, the true God is displaced, and life becomes a mess. That's the thought here. When we hold nothing back from God, God will hold back nothing that is necessary to accomplish his will and do his work.

We see an illustration of this principle and promised provision in the Old Testament book of 1 Kings. Following the Lord's faithful care of his prophet Elijah by ravens, which daily delivered bread and meat, God directed him to go to a town named Zarephath, where he would again be fed, this time by a poor widow. When Elijah arrived, he found the widow gathering sticks at the city gate and asked her for bread and water.

> So she said, "As the LORD your God lives, I
> do not have bread, only a handful of flour
> in a bin, and a little oil in a jar; and see, I
> am gathering a couple of sticks that I may
> go in and prepare it for myself and my son,
> that we may eat it, and die."

And Elijah said to her, "Do not fear; go and do as you have said, but make me a small cake from it first, and bring it to me; and afterward make some for yourself and your son. For thus says the LORD God of Israel: 'The bin of flour shall not be used up, nor shall the jar of oil run dry, until the day the LORD sends rain on the earth.'"

(1 Kings 17:12–14)

The widow did as God's prophet had directed her. She gave her last meal to him. What happened next? Her flour never ran out, and her oil flask never ran dry again. God provided for her needs. As she trusted the Lord by submitting to his messenger's message, she experienced what would later be promised in Matthew 6:33 by Jesus. She sought first the kingdom of God, and all her needs were added unto her. So it will be for us. When you and I give God and his work the proper place in our lives, everything else will fall into its proper place.

One Day at a Time

Let's return to Jesus' sermon.

> *Therefore do not worry about tomorrow, for*
> *tomorrow will worry about its own things.*
> *Sufficient for the day is its own trouble.*
> (Matthew 6:34)

Jesus knew his disciples were worried about the immediate, *today*, as well as about the next day, *tomorrow*. Therefore, his closing counsel to them was to live one day at a time, to restrict their concerns to today. It's as if Jesus is saying, "You know what? There's enough trouble in any given day for any of us to deal with. But if you're also going to borrow from tomorrow and bring it into today, then you're in double trouble."

The reason why we worry so much is because we worry too much. We worry two days at a time. In fact, some of us are so good at worrying we worry a week at a time. But Jesus tells us not to do that. To worry about tomorrow is unwise because it doesn't drain tomorrow of its sorrows, it only drains today of its strength. It's futile to worry about tomorrow.

We're not to worry about tomorrow because there is enough to deal with today without loading our plate from tomorrow's menu. Each day serves up enough trouble without picking a fight with the next day. The trouble with many of us is that we've got into an unhealthy and unholy habit of going out to meet trouble halfway. We're looking over the balcony of today into tomorrow, which has a debilitating effect and makes life unbearable.

There are two days we *don't* need to worry about: yesterday and tomorrow. Yesterday, because it's gone and not coming back; and tomorrow, because we're not sure if it's coming at all or what it holds. The problem is that some of us drag yesterday into today and others pull tomorrow into today, making life more difficult and less joyful. Wisdom informs us that we can only live one day at a time. God has appointed to each day its portion of pleasure and pain. As the old Swedish hymn says, especially in the last two lines of its verse:

Day by day and with each passing moment,
Strength I find to meet my trials here;
Trusting in my Father's wise bestowment,
I've no cause for worry or for fear.

He whose heart is kind beyond all measure
Gives unto each day what He deems best—
Lovingly, its part of pain and pleasure,
Mingling toil with peace and rest.

(Carolina Sandell, 1865)

In light of the hymnwriter's reminder and Jesus' teaching, we must not bring future troubles forward into today by being anxious. We must believe that God will still be God tomorrow, as he is today (Hebrews 13:8; Revelation 1:8). Tomorrow there will be enough grace for its own troubles. Grace cannot be borrowed or hoarded. The grace for tomorrow is not given today. So don't cross the proverbial bridge until you get there. Jesus said, "Sufficient for the day is its own trouble." God will give you grace to live one day at a time.

Conclusion

The church higher-ups in eighteenth-century England were stumped when the saintly John Fletcher of Madeley, John Wesley's "designated successor," refused the bishopric of Rochester. It was a plum position. Not quite understanding the refusal, and wondering if he was holding out for a better offer, they asked him if there was anything else he wanted. Within seconds his priorities were made crystal clear: "I want more grace," was his reply.[9]

We all want more grace, and we all need it, but the interesting thing is that God does not give us more grace until grace is needed. Even then, he gives grace only to the degree that we need it. We see this illustrated in the way God provided for the Israelites during their wilderness wanderings. Each morning they awoke to God's provision of sweet, flaky bread called "manna." However, God instructed them to gather only enough for that particular day. If they took more than was needed, reflecting their lack of trust in God to be faithful tomorrow, the extra they hoarded would spoil. What was God trying to teach them? He wanted them to rest in his promise to provide what was needed for each day (Exodus 16). Deuteronomy 33:25 reaffirms the same principle, as Moses says,

> As your days, so shall your strength be.

God will give us the strength we need to live each day—nothing more and nothing less.

God's provision of grace typically comes to us through prayer, as Hebrews 4:16 exhorts:

> Let us therefore come boldly to the throne
> of grace, that we may obtain mercy and
> find grace to help in time of need.

Interestingly, that last phrase could be translated, "grace for well-timed help." God's grace is for *now*; it contains a "best if used by" date.

More grace is what we all want and need, and it will be given in the perfect amount at the perfect time. Therefore, we can live today without anxiety, because the same Father who takes care of the birds of the air and the flowers of the field knows what we need before we even tell him. God will give grace and more grace, perfectly proportioned to cover our needs as we seek his kingdom first. Worry doesn't work, but God works all the time. So stop worrying. Start trusting, and begin resting.

PERSONAL APPLICATION PROJECTS

In a journal or notebook, work through the following application questions and projects.

Chapter 1

1. Read Proverbs 6:6–11. Compare these verses with James 4:13–17.

> » Is it always prideful to make plans for the future? Why or why not?

> » What godly attitudes should always accompany our planning?

> » What sinful motives or fleshly attitudes might get in the way of our practical application of God's wisdom?

> » In your journal or notebook, make a list of all the works you would like to accomplish in the future. Do any of your "future plans" remain uncommitted to the Lord? Take a few minutes to commit them to the Lord now.

2. Read Philippians 3:13–14.

> » In the spirit of "forgetting those things which are behind," is there anything in your past that is causing you anxiety? Are there hurts or sins that you need to talk to someone about—perhaps your pastor or another mature believer in your church? Are there sins you need to confess to God? To others?

> » What resolutions should you make in order to pursue Christ more fully?

> » Spend time in prayer. Tell the Lord about your hurts. Confess your sins. Commit your ways to him.

Chapter 2

1. In your journal or notebook, list the things that worry you the most right now.

> » Which of these are legitimate concerns, things that correspond to your personal responsibilities?

> » Which are distractions that are beyond your control?

> » Which of them has God already promised to take care of for you?

2. Read Romans 5:1–11.

>> Where does peace come from?

>> What are some of the works of God mentioned in this passage?

>> How has the love of God been made known to us?

>> How should you respond to the love of God in Jesus Christ?

Chapter 3

1. Read Philippians 4:6–7. Notice that the discipline of prayer, which brings the peace of God, includes thanksgiving. Section off a good number of pages at the back of your journal to begin a "Reasons to Be Thankful" list. Write down the specific works of God, and answers to prayer, for which you are thankful. Add to the list whenever more reasons come to mind.

2. Read Philippians 4:6–7 again, but this time also read verse 8.

>> Look up each adjective in a dictionary, Bible handbook, or concordance.

>> Compare this list to the characteristics of

Scripture mentioned in Psalm 19:7–11.

» How might the psalmist's prayer in 19:14 relate to Philippians 4:8?

» What adjustments do you need to make to your public and/or private Scripture-intake habits so that your mind may be renewed by biblical truth?

Chapter 4

1. Read Luke 10:38–42.

   » Why was Martha distracted? How did her anxiety provoke her to respond to Mary? To Jesus?

   » How did Jesus instruct Martha to combat her anxiety?

   » When you are anxious, how do you respond to others around you? Do you become frustrated with them? Do you sometimes sin against them with your words? What are the most common ways you are tempted to justify your frustration? Talk to the Lord about this, confessing whatever sins the Spirit brings to your mind.

» How important is "time with Jesus" to you? Do you spend time daily in the Scriptures and in prayer? If not, what changes do you need to make to your schedule?

2. Select a few Scriptures from the following list to memorize. Write them on 3x5 cards and place them where you will see them a few times a day.

» Matthew 6:26

» Isaiah 26:3

» Matthew 6:33

» Isaiah 64:4

» Lamentations 3:22–25

» 1 Peter 5:7

Where Can I Get More Help?

Books and Mini-Books

James, Joel, *Help! I Can't Handle All These Trials* (Wapwallopen, PA: Shepherd Press, 2016).

Kellemen, Bob, *Anxiety: Anatomy and Cure* (Phillipsburg, NJ: P&R, 2012).

MacArthur, John, *Anxiety Attacked* (Colorado Springs, CO: David C. Cook, 2012).

———, *Found: God's Peace* (Colorado Springs, CO: David C. Cook, 2015).

Newheiser, Jim, *Help! I Want to Change* (Wapwallopen, PA: Shepherd Press, 2014).

Scott, Stuart, *Anger, Anxiety, and Fear* (Bemidji, MN: Focus, 2009).

Wallace, Jocelyn, *Anxiety and Panic Attacks* (Greensboro, NC: New Growth Press, 2013).

Websites

Association of Certified Biblical Counselors, www.biblicalcounseling.com

Biblical Counseling Coalition, www.biblicalcounselingcoalition.org

Christian Counseling & Educational Foundation, www.ccef.org

ENDNOTES

1. Leon Morris, *The Gospel According to Matthew* (Grand Rapids, MI: Eerdmans, 1992), 157.

2. The phrase "respectable sin" was coined by Jerry Bridges in his excellent book *Respectable Sins* (Colorado Springs, CO: NavPress, 2007).

3. Quoted in Roy B. Zuck, *The Speaker's Quote Book* (Grand Rapids, MI: Kregel, 1997), 16.

4. Vance Havner, *The Vance Havner Notebook* (Grand Rapids, MI: Baker, 1989), 285.

5. Quoted in Iain H. Murray, *Wesley and Men Who Followed* (Carlisle, PA: Banner of Truth Trust, 2003), 8–9.

6. Quoted in Morris H. Chapman, *Jesus: Author and Finisher* (Nashville: Broadman, 1987), 45.

7. Sinclair Ferguson, *Kingdom Life in a Fallen World* (Colorado Springs, CO: NavPress, 1986), 179–180.

8. From Nicky Gumbel, *Challenging Lifestyle* (Eastbourne: Kingsway, 1996), 199.

9. Raymond Brown, *The Message of Deuteronomy* (Downers Grove, IL: InterVarsity Press, 1993), 60.

The Teaching Ministry of Philip De Courcy

Our Mission

At *Know the Truth*, we are fully devoted to teaching God's Word with boldness, clarity, and conviction using every technological means available.

Daily Radio Program

Each day, *Know the Truth* distributes the Bible teaching of Philip De Courcy across the U.S. on over 600 radio outlets. To find a radio station near you, visit https://www.ktt.org/broadcasts/stations-list.

Phone App

The *Know the Truth* podcast may easily be subscribed to through the KTT phone app. You can listen to daily broadcasts and previous teaching series anytime, and wherever you are, by downloading the app here:

https://www.ktt.org/broadcasts/subscribe-podcast.

Contact Know the Truth

- » Visit our website at www.ktt.org
- » Call: (888) 644-8811
- » Email: info@ktt.org
- » Write: Know The Truth | P.O. Box 30250 | Anaheim, CA 92809-0208

BOOKS IN THE HELP! SERIES INCLUDE...

More titles in preparation

For current listing go to: www.shepherdpress.com/lifeline

About Shepherd Press Publications

- » They are gospel driven.
- » They are heart focused.
- » They are life changing.

Our Invitation to You

We passionately believe that what we are publishing can be of benefit to you, your family, your friends, and your work colleagues. So we are inviting you to join our online mailing list so that we may reach out to you with news about our latest and forthcoming publications, and with special offers.

Visit:

www.shepherdpress.com/newsletter

and provide your name and email address.